AI-Driven Leadership

How Business Leaders Can Leverage AI to Transform Their Organizations

Hamid Oudi

Disclaimer

Copyright © 2024 Hamid Oudi, MyFalcon LTD
All rights reserved.

The framework presented in this book reflects the professional opinion of the author based on their experience working in the sector for the past 15 years. Any potential value estimates on business revenue and profit from AI/Data Science integration are derived from case studies for similar clients. However, these estimates should not be viewed as promises or guarantees for future outcomes.

Use of Case Studies:
Due to confidentiality agreements and privacy concerns, the real-world case studies discussed in this book are based on anonymized scenarios. The businesses and characters, such as Tom, Sophia, and Olivia, are fictional and are used to represent general challenges and solutions in AI adoption. These examples explain the art of the possible in AI applications and are not drawn from specific, real-life clients. No confidential details have been disclosed.

No part of this book may be reproduced, stored in a retrieval system, or transmitted in any form or by any means—electronic, mechanical, photocopying, recording, or otherwise—without the express written permission of the publisher.

Table of Contents

INTRODUCTION: LEADING THE CHARGE IN THE AGE OF AI 2

CHAPTER 1: THE NEED FOR AI IN BUSINESS 5

    THE LEADERSHIP IMPERATIVE IN AI ADOPTION 6
    AI ADOPTION CHALLENGES: THE ROADBLOCKS YOU'LL FACE 7
    THE COMPETITIVE ADVANTAGE OF AI: WHY YOU CAN'T AFFORD TO WAIT 10
    THE LEADERSHIP ROLE IN AI TRANSFORMATION 11

CHAPTER 2: UNDERSTANDING AI AND ITS IMPACT ON BUSINESSES .. 13

    THE CORE TECHNOLOGIES BEHIND AI 14
        Machine Learning (ML) 14
        Natural Language Processing (NLP) 15
        Robotic Process Automation (RPA) 15
        Generative AI (GenAI) 16
        Large Language Models (LLMs) 16
    AI'S BUSINESS APPLICATIONS: FROM MARKETING TO OPERATIONS 17
        Customer Service 17
        Sales and Marketing 18
        Supply Chain and Logistics 18
        Finance and Risk Management 19
    AI IN ACTION: REAL-WORLD BUSINESS SUCCESS STORIES 19
        Case Study 1: Healthcare Diagnostics 19
        Case Study 2: Retail Personalization 20
    THE COMPETITIVE EDGE OF AI: WHY YOU CAN'T AFFORD TO WAIT 20

CHAPTER 3: BUILDING AN AI-READY ORGANIZATION 22

    STEP 1: ASSESSING AI READINESS 22
        Data Infrastructure 23
        Organizational Culture 23
        Technical Readiness 24
        Leadership Alignment 25
    STEP 2: ALIGNING LEADERSHIP AND TEAMS 25

STEP 3: FOSTERING A CULTURE OF INNOVATION 26
STEP 4: BUILDING THE RIGHT DATA INFRASTRUCTURE 27
STEP 5: DEVELOPING AI TALENT AND SKILLS 28
STEP 6: START SMALL, SCALE FAST 29
STEP 7: MEASURE AND OPTIMIZE 30

CHAPTER 4: ALIGNING TEAMS AND MANAGING AI PROJECTS 32

DEFINING CLEAR GOALS AND SUCCESS METRICS 33
MANAGING CROSS-DEPARTMENTAL COLLABORATION AND COMMUNICATION 35
BUILDING THE RIGHT AI TEAM: SKILLS AND COLLABORATION 36
OVERCOMING RESISTANCE TO AI ADOPTION 37
ENSURING ALIGNMENT BETWEEN AI AND BUSINESS STRATEGY 38

CHAPTER 5: AI LEADERSHIP AND DECISION MAKING 40

BALANCING SHORT-TERM GOALS WITH LONG-TERM AI STRATEGY 41
UNDERSTANDING THE ETHICAL IMPLICATIONS OF AI DECISIONS 43
LEADING WITH EMPATHY: BUILDING TRUST AROUND AI 45
EMPOWERING DATA-DRIVEN DECISION MAKING 47
STRATEGIC DECISION MAKING: ALIGNING AI WITH BUSINESS GOALS 48

CHAPTER 6: NAVIGATING AI IMPLEMENTATION CHALLENGES 50

CHALLENGE 1: DATA QUALITY AND AVAILABILITY 51
CHALLENGE 2: OVERCOMING TECHNICAL DEBT AND INTEGRATION ISSUES 53
CHALLENGE 3: ETHICAL CONCERNS, PRIVACY ISSUES, AND REGULATORY COMPLIANCE 55
CHALLENGE 4: MANAGING STAKEHOLDER EXPECTATIONS 57
CHALLENGE 5: OVERCOMING RESISTANCE TO AI ADOPTION 59

CHAPTER 7: THE FUTURE OF AI IN BUSINESS AND LEADERSHIP 61

AI AND THE NEXT FRONTIER: EMERGING TECHNOLOGIES 62
  Generative AI (GenAI) 62
  Autonomous Systems 63
  Edge Computing and Real-Time AI 64
  AI-Driven Predictive Analytics 65

PREPARING FOR AI IN THE LONG-TERM: BUILDING A SUSTAINABLE AI STRATEGY ... 67
   Upskilling and Reskilling the Workforce 67
   AI Governance and Ethical Standards... 68
   Building a Long-Term AI Roadmap 69
PREPARING FOR AN AI-DRIVEN FUTURE: BUILDING ADAPTABILITY 70

CHAPTER 8: CONCLUSION – LEADING AI-DRIVEN CHANGE 72

THE ROADMAP FOR AI ADOPTION: FROM STRATEGY TO EXECUTION 72
THE ROLE OF AI LEADERSHIP IN THE FUTURE 76
   Taking Charge of AI-Driven Change 77

ACKNOWLEDGEMENT 81
ABOUT THE AUTHOR.. 82

Introduction: Leading the Charge in the Age of AI

What was once a buzzword is now driving the most impactful innovations in industries across the globe. AI is no longer confined to tech giants or cutting-edge startups—it's being adopted by businesses of all sizes and industries, from healthcare to retail, from logistics to finance. But here's the reality: AI adoption isn't just about technology—it's about leadership.

As AI continues to reshape the way we work and do business, the question is no longer whether AI will become a central part of your company's strategy, but how quickly you can adapt and lead your organization through this transformation. It's a challenge that requires vision, strategy, and, most importantly, strong leadership.

As a business leader, you hold the key to unlocking the potential of AI within your organization. But understanding AI's capabilities, overcoming obstacles, and aligning your teams with AI's potential can feel daunting, especially if you don't have a technical background. You might feel overwhelmed by the complexities of the technology or unsure of how to translate AI into something that will drive measurable business outcomes. And that's where this guide comes in.

This book is for business leaders like you—CEOs, executives, and managers—who understand the importance of AI but may not know exactly where to start. This guide is here to help you navigate the world of AI adoption and leadership, providing you with practical advice, real-world examples, and actionable frameworks that you can implement in your own organization.

For the past 15 years, I've been at the forefront of AI and data science, helping businesses of all sizes integrate AI technologies to drive efficiency, enhance customer experiences, and increase profitability. As a Data Scientist and Machine Learning Engineer, I've witnessed firsthand the transformative power of AI. But I've also seen the challenges—technical hurdles, organizational resistance, and cultural barriers—that often stand in the way of successful AI adoption. I've worked with executives and teams to address these obstacles and guide them through the complexities of AI implementation.

Through this book, I will share the lessons I've learned, both from my own experiences and from working with organizations across a range of industries. You'll discover that AI adoption is not just a technical challenge, but a strategic one that requires a shift in mindset, culture, and leadership. As you read through these chapters, you'll learn how to:

- Build an AI-ready organization, from aligning teams to fostering a culture of innovation.

- Lead AI projects that drive business value and measurable outcomes.

- Overcome resistance and challenges that often accompany AI adoption.

- Ensure your AI strategy aligns with your long-term business goals, keeping your organization competitive in a rapidly changing landscape.

AI is already here. It's reshaping industries, improving efficiencies, and driving innovation. The businesses that will thrive in the AI era are those that embrace it, not just from a technological standpoint, but as a strategic tool for growth. But adopting AI is not just about investing in the right technology—it's about having the leadership, vision, and strategy to successfully integrate AI into your business.

In the following chapters, we'll explore the key steps every leader must take to guide their teams through AI adoption and ensure that AI becomes a strategic asset. Whether you are taking your first steps with AI or scaling AI projects across your organization, this guide will provide you with the tools and frameworks you need to succeed in the age of AI.

So, let's dive in—because AI isn't just the future of business; it's the present. And the time to lead with AI is now.

Chapter 1: The Need for AI in Business

In the early days of artificial intelligence, the concept seemed distant—a shiny technology reserved for tech giants and cutting-edge innovators. AI was often associated with science fiction or, at best, something for the future. But the future is now, and AI is at the heart of the most transformative shifts in the business landscape today.

Take Sarah, for example. Sarah is the CEO of a mid-sized e-commerce company that has experienced steady growth. She knows that the competitive landscape is changing, but she's also aware that the pressure to innovate is constant. Sarah noticed her competitors were using AI in ways that were making them faster, smarter, and more efficient. AI-driven predictive analytics, chatbots, and automated inventory management were becoming commonplace, offering enhanced customer experiences and streamlined operations.

At first, Sarah thought that AI was something only big players like Amazon or Walmart could afford. But as she dug deeper into AI, Sarah realized that businesses of all sizes could harness its potential. It wasn't just a tool for big tech companies; it was a tool for transformation, ready to be utilized by businesses with a vision for innovation.

Sarah's story reflects a larger shift happening globally. AI is no longer a luxury or something for the distant future—it's here, and businesses that fail to adopt it risk being left behind. Companies that embrace AI can automate routine tasks, gain real-time insights into customer behaviour, optimize operations, and, ultimately, drive growth and profitability. On the flip side, companies that don't adopt AI run the risk of being outpaced by more agile, AI-driven competitors.

But there's a catch—AI adoption isn't just about technology. It's about leadership. And that's where this book comes in.

The Leadership Imperative in AI Adoption

As Sarah learned, AI adoption is not simply a matter of installing a new tool or technology. It requires a strategic shift, and that shift starts with leadership. Business leaders must create a vision for AI, align their teams, and foster an environment where AI can thrive. It's not just about understanding algorithms or data models—leaders must guide the entire organization through the changes that AI will bring.

AI doesn't just change processes; it transforms organizational cultures. It challenges old ways of thinking and requires new skill sets across the workforce. For Sarah, the transition to AI wasn't just about implementing technology; it was about inspiring her team to see the value of AI and how it could support their goals. AI would allow them to personalize customer experiences, predict inventory needs, and respond to customer queries 24/7 with chatbots. But none of this would happen if the team wasn't on board and aligned.

This is where leadership plays a critical role. Leaders must build a culture that embraces change and innovation. They must communicate clearly about the potential of AI, address any fears or misunderstandings, and provide the necessary training and resources. Only when leadership is engaged can AI be adopted successfully across the organization.

AI Adoption Challenges: The Roadblocks You'll Face

As much as AI promises to transform businesses, it doesn't come without challenges. Many leaders are eager to adopt AI, but they encounter roadblocks that slow down or even derail their efforts. These challenges aren't necessarily technical in nature—often, they are cultural, organizational, or leadership-related.

Take John, for instance, who runs a regional logistics company. John had heard about AI's potential in route optimization and inventory management, but when he began to explore the possibilities, he quickly realized that his company wasn't ready for the transformation. The data was fragmented, teams were siloed, and many employees were resistant to the changes that AI might bring. While John was excited about the potential of AI, he found that the biggest hurdle wasn't the technology—it was overcoming resistance to change.

As a leader, John had to navigate this resistance, foster a culture of innovation, and build the right infrastructure to make AI adoption possible. The experience taught him an important lesson: AI isn't just a technology issue—it's a leadership challenge.

Some of the most common obstacle's organizations face in AI adoption include:

- **Data Quality**: AI is powered by data, but many organizations struggle with poor data quality. Without accurate, clean data, AI models can't perform effectively. Leaders must address data governance and ensure their data infrastructure is ready for AI integration.

- **Cultural Resistance**: Employees often resist AI adoption due to fear of job displacement or a lack of understanding. Leaders must engage their teams, address concerns, and build trust in AI systems.

- **Lack of Skills**: Many organizations face a skills gap when adopting AI. Leaders must invest in upskilling their teams, building internal AI expertise, and fostering a culture of continuous learning.

- **Integration with Legacy Systems**: AI solutions often need to integrate with existing systems, which can be a complex and costly endeavour. Leaders must plan for seamless integration and prioritize projects that offer the most significant return on investment.

The Competitive Advantage of AI: Why You Can't Afford to Wait

AI is no longer a luxury—it's a competitive necessity. The businesses that are leading the charge in AI adoption are reaping the rewards: lower costs, improved customer experiences, enhanced decision-making, and the ability to adapt to changing market conditions in real-time.

Take, for example, a major retail chain that integrated AI into its inventory management system. By using predictive analytics, the company was able to reduce stockouts by 30% and cut excess inventory by 25%. This wasn't just a technological improvement—it was a game-changer for the business, helping them stay ahead of the competition.

AI is also unlocking new opportunities for innovation. Companies that embrace AI can tap into new business models, create more personalized customer experiences, and even discover entirely new revenue streams. AI empowers businesses to make data-driven decisions faster and more accurately, ultimately giving them a distinct competitive edge.

But AI's potential isn't just about improving what's already been done—it's about creating entirely new ways of doing business. With AI, businesses can automate routine tasks, predict future trends, and innovate in ways that were previously unimaginable.

The Leadership Role in AI Transformation

As this chapter has illustrated, AI adoption is not just a technological issue—it's a leadership challenge. Leaders like Sarah, John, and countless others are at the helm of AI transformation, guiding their organizations through the complexities of AI adoption. The question for business leaders isn't whether AI should be embraced—it's how quickly can you adapt and lead your teams through the transition?

AI has the power to change how we do business—but only if we lead with vision, strategy, and the right mindset. In the chapters ahead, we will explore the steps you can take to build an AI-ready organization, align your teams, and drive successful AI adoption. We'll cover the practical strategies, challenges, and tools that will help you integrate AI into your business and stay ahead of the curve.

Key Takeaways:

- AI is not a luxury—it's a competitive necessity.

- AI adoption is driven by leadership, not just technology.

- Leaders must overcome cultural resistance, invest in data quality, and upskill their teams to successfully implement AI.

- AI adoption offers businesses a unique opportunity to innovate, improve efficiency, and gain a competitive edge.

Chapter 2: Understanding AI and Its Impact on Businesses

When the term **artificial intelligence (AI)** is mentioned, many businesses leaders' picture futuristic robots or complex scientific concepts that seem too abstract or advanced for their company. But AI is not just a technological dream—it's already here, and it's influencing the way companies run their operations, communicate with customers, and innovate in ways that weren't possible just a few years ago.

At its core, AI refers to systems or machines that can perform tasks that would normally require human intelligence. This includes tasks like recognizing speech, making predictions based on data, or solving complex problems. However, to fully harness AI's potential in business, it's important to break down its core components and understand how these technologies can be applied practically.

Let's start by considering **Emily**, a marketing director at a fast-growing e-commerce company. Emily was initially overwhelmed by the possibilities of AI but soon realized that it could transform her marketing strategy. Rather than relying solely on historical data or guesswork, Emily's team adopted machine learning (ML) algorithms to predict customer preferences and behaviour in real-time. By analysing past interactions and purchase patterns, the system could suggest products tailored to individual shoppers, which led to a dramatic increase in customer engagement and sales.

This practical application of machine learning is just one example of how AI can drive business success. But to truly understand AI's impact on your organization, you need to grasp the various AI technologies that power these systems.

The Core Technologies Behind AI

The world of AI is vast, and it can be overwhelming to navigate the technical terms and concepts. But it doesn't need to be intimidating. Here, we'll break down the most important AI technologies in a way that makes them easy to understand—and more importantly, shows how you can use them to drive business growth.

Machine Learning (ML)

At the heart of many AI applications, **machine learning** is a method of data analysis that automates analytical model building. It uses algorithms that learn from past data and make decisions based on it. In business, ML is often used for predictive analytics, customer segmentation, demand forecasting, and personalized recommendations. The more data these models process, the better they become at predicting outcomes, which enables businesses to continuously optimize their operations. For example, a retail company might use ML to analyse purchasing patterns and predict which products are likely to be in demand during the next season, optimizing inventory and reducing waste. The system becomes smarter over time as it is fed more data, improving its predictions and helping businesses stay ahead of trends.

Natural Language Processing (NLP)

NLP allows machines to understand, interpret, and respond to human language in a way that is both meaningful and valuable. NLP powers technologies like chatbots, virtual assistants, sentiment analysis, and voice recognition. It's a key part of enhancing customer service, personalizing experiences, and even improving internal communications. A customer service team might use NLP to deploy AI-powered chatbots that can handle a range of inquiries, such as order status, returns, or product recommendations. This automation allows the company to offer 24/7 support, reducing response times and increasing customer satisfaction. In fact, some companies are now able to resolve most inquiries without human intervention, significantly improving operational efficiency.

Robotic Process Automation (RPA)

While **RPA** is not technically a form of AI, it often works together with AI technologies to automate repetitive, rule-based tasks. RPA is used in scenarios where simple tasks such as data entry, invoice processing, and report generation need to be automated to save time and reduce human error. For example, a finance department may use RPA to automate invoice processing. This frees up employees to focus on more strategic tasks while ensuring that all invoices are processed accurately and on time.

Generative AI (GenAI)

Generative AI refers to a class of AI models that can generate new content—whether it's text, images, audio, or even video. Unlike traditional AI, which primarily analyses and predicts based on data, **Generative AI** creates new data that closely resembles what it was trained on. One of the most famous examples of generative AI is **GPT-3** (Generative Pretrained Transformer 3), a language model capable of producing human-like text. Businesses are already using GenAI for a wide range of applications, including content creation, customer support, and even generating code for software development. Imagine a content team in a publishing company using **GenAI** to generate blog posts or marketing copy. Instead of starting from scratch, the AI can create a draft in minutes, which the team can then refine. Similarly, creative industries are using AI to generate art or video content, significantly reducing production time and costs.

Large Language Models (LLMs)

A subset of Generative AI, **Large Language Models** like GPT-3 and **BERT** (Bidirectional Encoder Representations from Transformers) are designed to understand, generate, and interact with human language. These models have been trained on massive datasets containing vast amounts of text from the internet, allowing them to perform a variety of language-related tasks, from translation and summarization to question-answering and creative writing.

In businesses, LLMs are being used for applications such as customer service, where they can provide human-like responses to customer inquiries, or in content creation, where they can generate product descriptions or social media posts. Their ability to process and generate natural language text has made them a powerful tool in automating communication and content generation.

AI's Business Applications: From Marketing to Operations

AI is not just a tool for tech companies—it is transforming businesses across every industry. Here are some key areas where AI is having a profound impact:

Customer Service

With NLP and GenAI, AI-driven chatbots and virtual assistants can offer real-time assistance to customers, providing quick answers to questions and automating routine tasks. For example, a telecom company might deploy a virtual assistant to handle customer inquiries about service outages, billing, or technical support, allowing human agents to focus on more complex issues.

Sales and Marketing

AI is revolutionizing how businesses approach sales and marketing. Through **predictive analytics** and **personalization algorithms**, companies can segment customers more accurately, predict buying behaviours, and tailor marketing campaigns in real-time. An AI model trained on past purchase behaviour might recommend specific products to a customer, increasing the likelihood of a purchase.

For example, a global fashion brand used AI-powered recommendation engines to personalize product suggestions for every visitor to their website. This resulted in a 20% increase in online sales as customers received tailored suggestions based on their preferences and browsing history.

Supply Chain and Logistics

AI can analyse vast amounts of supply chain data to forecast demand, optimize routes, and manage inventory more efficiently. Companies like Amazon and UPS use AI to predict delivery times, optimize packaging, and route deliveries more efficiently. AI-powered predictive maintenance also ensures that equipment is maintained before it breaks down, minimizing costly downtime.

In one case, a logistics company adopted AI to predict and optimize delivery routes, resulting in a 15% reduction in fuel costs and a 20% reduction in delivery times.

Finance and Risk Management

In the financial industry, AI is used to detect fraud, assess risk, and automate tasks such as loan processing. For example, banks use machine learning algorithms to analyse transaction data in real-time to flag fraudulent activity. Similarly, AI is used to automate the approval process for loans, providing faster responses to customers while reducing the risk of human error.

AI in Action: Real-World Business Success Stories

Case Study 1: Healthcare Diagnostics

A healthcare provider used AI-powered tools to assist in medical imaging, allowing radiologists to detect early-stage diseases such as cancer. The AI system was able to identify abnormalities in X-rays and MRIs with a level of accuracy comparable to that of human specialists, speeding up diagnoses and reducing errors. In the first year, the hospital saw a 25% reduction in diagnostic errors, and patient outcomes improved significantly.

Case Study 2: Retail Personalization

A global retail chain implemented AI to enhance customer personalization. By analysing customer browsing and purchasing history, the AI system was able to recommend products to each shopper, tailored to their tastes and preferences. This personalized approach led to a 30% increase in average order value and a 15% improvement in customer retention.

The Competitive Edge of AI: Why You Can't Afford to Wait

AI is not just a tool for improving efficiency—it's a competitive advantage. The companies that are leading the charge in AI are not only automating tasks but are using AI to innovate, enhance customer experiences, and gain deeper insights into their operations. Businesses that fail to integrate AI risk falling behind.

As we've seen with Emily's story, AI is about more than just adopting new technologies—it's about using those technologies to drive growth, improve customer relationships, and transform how business is done. AI offers an opportunity to be more agile, more innovative, and more data driven.

Key Takeaways:

- AI isn't just a buzzword; it's already reshaping industries and improving business operations.

- Core AI technologies like ML, NLP, and Generative AI are enabling businesses to predict customer behaviour, automate routine tasks, and enhance personalization.

- AI is being applied in every business function, from marketing and customer service to supply chain management and finance.

- Companies that adopt AI are gaining a competitive edge in efficiency, innovation, and customer satisfaction.

Chapter 3: Building an AI-Ready Organization

When Sarah, the CEO of the mid-sized e-commerce company, decided to integrate AI into her business, she quickly realized something critical: **AI adoption is not a one-size-fits-all solution.** It's not enough to simply purchase AI tools and expect instant transformation. To be successful, AI needs to be woven into the fabric of the organization—aligned with business goals, integrated into workflows, and embraced by the team.

The very first thing Sarah did was to assess whether her company was ready for AI. AI is a powerful tool, but it's only effective when the organization can fully leverage it. Sarah understood that adopting AI would require changes across several dimensions of the business. It wasn't just about installing software; it was about reshaping the company's processes, data infrastructure, culture, and leadership approach to accommodate and capitalize on AI. She broke this down into a step-by-step approach.

Step 1: Assessing AI Readiness

Before diving headfirst into AI adoption, Sarah took the time to conduct a comprehensive assessment of the organization's readiness. This meant looking at several key areas to ensure the company could not only support AI but truly benefit from it.

Data Infrastructure

AI thrives on data, but data must be **clean, organized, and accessible**. Sarah's team had accumulated vast amounts of customer data, but it was fragmented across different departments. Sales data was in one system, customer service logs in another, and website browsing patterns were stored separately. This data was unstructured, meaning it wasn't formatted or labelled in a way that AI models could immediately use.

To address this, Sarah invested in a **centralized data platform**—a **data lake**—where all customer data could be stored in one place. She also focused on **data governance** by setting up systems to clean and validate the data, ensuring that the information used for AI models was consistent, accurate, and up to date. With a solid data foundation, Sarah's company was now able to use AI to unlock valuable insights and predictions.

Organizational Culture

AI adoption isn't just about technology; it's about cultural change. Sarah realized that her company needed to build a culture that welcomed innovation, embraced change, and encouraged experimentation. Many employees were used to traditional workflows and processes, and AI was often viewed as an unnecessary complication or a threat to job security.

To overcome this, Sarah held **company-wide workshops** to introduce AI, explain its potential benefits, and address concerns. She emphasized that AI was a tool to enhance human capabilities, not replace them. For example, AI could automate repetitive tasks, allowing employees to focus on more creative and strategic endeavours. Sarah also fostered a sense of **ownership** over AI projects by forming cross-functional teams that included people from different departments—marketing, IT, operations, and customer service—who could collaborate and share their insights on AI's application in their areas.

Technical Readiness

Sarah's company had a basic IT infrastructure, but it wasn't optimized for the computational power required by AI models. She realized that AI projects would need robust computing power and resources to store and process large volumes of data.

Sarah decided to invest in **cloud computing platforms** like AWS and Google Cloud, which offered scalable solutions for data storage, processing, and AI model training. These platforms allowed her to use high-performance servers without needing to build expensive on-premises infrastructure. She also began the process of recruiting **data scientists, machine learning engineers**, and other AI experts who could handle the technical aspects of deploying and managing AI models.

Leadership Alignment

The next critical factor in AI adoption was getting her leadership team on the same page. Sarah knew that AI initiatives would need to be championed at the top level, and the leadership team had to understand the potential value of AI. She made sure that all the department heads, from marketing to supply chain management, saw AI as a strategic asset.

To achieve this, Sarah invited **AI consultants** to educate the leadership team on the applications of AI in their respective fields. They also discussed potential use cases for AI, such as predictive analytics for customer behaviour and automation of inventory management. This created alignment and excitement within the leadership team, setting the stage for broad organizational support.

Step 2: Aligning Leadership and Teams

Once Sarah had assessed the organization's readiness, the next step was ensuring that leadership and teams were aligned in their vision for AI. This alignment would provide the momentum necessary to drive AI initiatives forward.

Leaders in every department needed to understand **how AI could benefit their teams** and **how to integrate it into their workflows**. For instance, Sarah's **marketing team** was keen to leverage AI to improve customer segmentation and personalization, while the **customer service department** was excited about using AI-powered chatbots to handle routine inquiries and free up human agents for more complex tasks.

Sarah began by organizing regular meetings with the leadership team to clarify the goals of AI adoption, establish expectations, and **define success metrics**. These meetings fostered an environment where leadership could ask questions, voice concerns, and brainstorm new ways to use AI. They discussed the measurable business outcomes they hoped to achieve, such as increasing customer retention, optimizing inventory, and improving customer satisfaction.

Sarah also appointed **AI champions** in each department. These champions were responsible for coordinating AI initiatives within their teams, ensuring that everyone understood the goals, benefits, and implementation steps. The champions worked closely with the IT and AI teams to make sure that technical requirements were aligned with business goals, making the process smoother for everyone.

Step 3: Fostering a Culture of Innovation

As Sarah discovered, AI adoption goes together with fostering a culture of innovation. Without the right cultural mindset, AI initiatives can fall flat, no matter how powerful the technology is. Sarah wanted her company to be agile, open to experimentation, and willing to iterate on ideas quickly—values that are essential in AI development.

To build this culture, Sarah began promoting **cross-functional collaboration**. AI projects often require input from various departments, from data scientists to business analysts to operational leaders. By bringing people from different areas together, Sarah was able to create diverse teams that could tackle AI challenges from multiple perspectives.

Additionally, Sarah encouraged a **fail-fast, learn-fast mentality**. She knew that AI development often involves trial and error. AI models may not always perform perfectly on the first try, but if teams learned from their mistakes and iterated quickly, they would achieve better results over time. To reinforce this, Sarah ensured that employees had the time and resources to experiment, whether through pilot projects or dedicated innovation labs.

Step 4: Building the Right Data Infrastructure

AI cannot function without data, and for AI to be effective, the data must be of high quality. One of Sarah's first major challenges was addressing the **data silos** within her company. Data was being collected from multiple sources—website traffic, sales transactions, customer feedback—but it was scattered across different departments and systems. For AI to work, Sarah needed to bring this data together in a unified, accessible way.

She began by **centralizing the data** in a company-wide **data lake**, a repository that stores raw data in its native format until it's needed. With this data in one place, Sarah's team could access it easily, and AI models could analyse it more efficiently. She also introduced **data cleaning and validation tools** to ensure the information used for AI was accurate and consistent.

Another key part of building the right data infrastructure was ensuring that the data could be processed quickly. Sarah implemented **real-time data streaming** solutions to allow her AI models to analyse data as it was being generated. This capability was crucial for use cases like predictive analytics, where real-time insights are necessary to drive timely decisions.

Step 5: Developing AI Talent and Skills

Sarah knew that for AI to succeed, her company needed **talent**—specialists who could build and maintain AI models, understand complex algorithms, and extract actionable insights from data. She realized that this talent was scarce and expensive, so she decided to take a two-pronged approach: **upskilling existing employees** and **recruiting new talent**.

She launched an **AI Academy** within the company to train employees on data science, machine learning, and AI technologies. This allowed team members to learn from experts, complete hands-on projects, and develop AI skills at their own pace. The academy was open to employees from various departments, fostering a culture of cross-functional AI expertise.

In parallel, Sarah's HR team worked to **recruit data scientists, machine learning engineers**, and other AI specialists. She focused on attracting individuals who were not just technically proficient, but also passionate about AI and eager to contribute to the company's AI vision.

Step 6: Start Small, Scale Fast

With everything in place, Sarah was ready to begin implementing AI. She understood that AI adoption could be overwhelming, so she decided to **start small** with a **pilot project**. The marketing team, for example, started with an AI-powered recommendation engine to suggest products based on customer behaviour. This project was manageable, achievable, and allowed Sarah to demonstrate the value of AI without risking too much.

The pilot project was a success. It provided measurable results, like increased sales and improved customer engagement, which proved that AI could deliver tangible benefits. With this success in hand, Sarah quickly expanded AI initiatives to other departments, from customer service automation to predictive inventory management.

Step 7: Measure and Optimize

Sarah was committed to **continuous improvement**. She set up **KPIs** (Key Performance Indicators) to measure the success of AI initiatives, such as customer satisfaction scores, cost reductions, and revenue growth. She also created a **feedback loop** that allowed employees to provide input on AI systems, ensuring that the company was always optimizing and refining its AI tools.

Key Takeaways:

- **Assess AI readiness** by evaluating your organization's data infrastructure, culture, leadership alignment, and technical capabilities.

- **Foster a culture of innovation** by encouraging collaboration, experimentation, and a willingness to learn from failures.

- **Build strong data infrastructure** with centralized data storage, real-time processing, and robust data governance to ensure AI models can perform effectively.

- **Develop AI talent** by upskilling employees and hiring specialists who can help drive AI initiatives.

- **Start with small projects**, measure success, and scale AI adoption gradually across the organization.

Chapter 4: Aligning Teams and Managing AI Projects

When Sarah decided to launch her company's first AI initiative—predictive analytics for customer behaviour—she knew that success wasn't just about implementing the technology. The real challenge lay in coordinating her teams, aligning their efforts, and ensuring that the AI project would meet the company's strategic goals.

AI projects are unlike traditional projects. They are inherently cross-functional, involving collaboration between various departments like IT, marketing, sales, data science, and customer service. Unlike a standard software development project, where the scope and goals may be well-defined from the start, AI projects are often iterative. As such, managing AI projects requires a level of flexibility and communication that can sometimes be difficult to maintain in larger organizations.

Sarah's first step was to identify the key stakeholders involved in the project. She established a **cross-functional team** with representatives from marketing (to understand customer needs), IT (for infrastructure), and data science (to build and refine the models). Having the right mix of skills and expertise on the team was crucial to the project's success. Each member brought unique insights that would shape how AI was deployed.

However, getting the team aligned wasn't easy. Many members had different expectations about what the project could achieve. The marketing team was excited about the potential for personalization, while the IT team was more focused on the technical challenges. The data science team was eager to test out advanced algorithms, but they had to ensure that the model would deliver tangible business value.

To address these different perspectives, Sarah facilitated regular meetings to ensure all stakeholders were on the same page. These meetings weren't just about progress updates—they were an opportunity for team members to voice concerns, share ideas, and brainstorm solutions together. By creating an open and collaborative environment, Sarah ensured that everyone was working toward the same goals and had a clear understanding of the project's potential impact on the business.

Defining Clear Goals and Success Metrics

One of the most important aspects of managing any AI project is defining what success looks like. Unlike traditional projects where success is often measured by whether the project was delivered on time and within budget, AI projects require more nuanced metrics. For Sarah's AI initiative, success wasn't just about building a predictive model—it was about how well that model improved customer engagement and increased sales.

Sarah worked with her leadership team to set clear, measurable objectives for the project. These objectives were rooted in the company's strategic goals. They identified key performance indicators (KPIs) such as:

- **Conversion Rate**: How many customers who received personalized recommendations made a purchase.

- **Customer Retention**: Did the recommendations improve repeat purchases and loyalty?

- **Revenue Growth**: Was there a measurable increase in sales tied directly to AI-driven recommendations?

These KPIs allowed the team to measure the effectiveness of the AI model in real terms, ensuring that the project was aligned with the business's overall objectives. Sarah also emphasized that the AI model wasn't a "set it and forget it" solution. It would need continuous monitoring, testing, and optimization to remain effective.

As the project progressed, Sarah and her team adjusted their strategy based on these metrics. When they found that the initial recommendations were less effective than anticipated, they used the feedback from the KPIs to refine the model. This iterative approach allowed the team to continuously improve the AI solution and adapt to changing customer preferences.

Managing Cross-Departmental Collaboration and Communication

AI projects inherently require collaboration across departments, which can be challenging in organizations where teams are used to working in silos. For Sarah, this meant ensuring that communication remained open and transparent between the business units and the technical teams.

One key challenge Sarah faced was bridging the gap between the **technical teams** (data scientists and machine learning engineers) and the **non-technical teams** (marketing and operations). The AI team was focused on developing the best model possible, but they needed the marketing team's input to ensure the recommendations aligned with customer behaviour. On the other hand, marketing was eager to see results quickly, but they didn't fully understand the technical complexities involved in training AI models.

To resolve this, Sarah instituted a system of regular updates and check-ins. These weren't just formal reports; they were discussions designed to bring both sides together and ensure everyone had a shared understanding of what was happening at every stage.

For example, Sarah's team regularly shared progress with the marketing department, explaining how the AI model was trained and what variables it was using to make predictions. In return, the marketing team provided real-world feedback on how the recommendations were performing in live campaigns. This feedback loop helped the data scientists fine-tune the model and improve its predictions. It also kept the marketing team engaged and invested in the project's success.

Sarah learned that one of the most important aspects of leading AI projects is ensuring that both technical and non-technical teams **speak the same language**. Everyone needs to understand the project's goals and how their individual contributions fit into the bigger picture.

Building the Right AI Team: Skills and Collaboration

AI projects require a blend of technical and business skills. While data scientists, machine learning engineers, and software developers are essential for building AI models, business experts are needed to ensure that the AI is solving the right problems and delivering value to the business.

Sarah's team was successful in part because it had a diverse mix of talent. She made sure to include **data scientists** who were proficient in machine learning and **business analysts** who could translate AI insights into actionable strategies for marketing and operations.

In addition, Sarah recognized that the AI team wasn't just about having the right technical skills—it was about fostering a collaborative mindset. AI projects can be complex, and team members need to be adaptable and open to learning from each other. By encouraging a **culture of collaboration**, Sarah ensured that everyone—from technical experts to business leaders—was contributing to the success of the AI project.

Sarah's approach also involved **continuous training** for her team. AI is a fast-evolving field, and Sarah made sure her data scientists were up to date on the latest algorithms, best practices, and tools. She also encouraged her business teams to learn more about AI, so they could better understand how to leverage the technology in their day-to-day work.

Overcoming Resistance to AI Adoption

One of the greatest challenges Sarah faced was overcoming **resistance to change** within the organization. Many employees were sceptical about AI and worried about the impact it would have on their jobs. Some feared that automation would lead to job cuts, while others didn't fully understand how AI could improve their work.

Sarah addressed these concerns by being transparent and involving employees in the process. She communicated openly about how AI would be used to enhance their roles, not replace them. For example, AI could automate routine customer service tasks, but it wouldn't replace human agents. Instead, it would allow customer service representatives to focus on more complex issues, like building relationships with customers or solving intricate problems.

Sarah also encouraged a **growth mindset** throughout the organization. She promoted AI as a tool for employees to grow their skills and improve efficiency. Rather than seeing AI as a threat, Sarah's team began to see it to work smarter, not harder.

Ensuring Alignment Between AI and Business Strategy

Sarah knew that for AI to succeed, it couldn't be an isolated initiative. AI must be integrated with the company's overall business strategy. This meant aligning AI projects with the company's long-term goals and ensuring that AI initiatives directly supported the broader mission of the business.

For example, while the marketing team was focused on personalization, Sarah ensured that AI initiatives were also driving efficiency in other areas of the business, such as supply chain management and inventory control. By linking AI efforts across departments, Sarah created a **holistic approach** to AI adoption, ensuring that the technology was having a wide-reaching impact on the company.

Key Takeaways:

- **Cross-functional collaboration** is essential for successful AI projects. Involve technical and business teams from the start and ensure open, ongoing communication.

- **Define success metrics** early on, based on clear business objectives. Success isn't just about building a model—it's about delivering measurable business value.

- **Foster a culture of experimentation** and iteration. AI models need constant refinement and feedback from the business side to remain effective.

- **Build the right AI team** by combining technical skills with business expertise. Encourage continuous learning and a collaborative mindset.

- **Overcome resistance to AI adoption** by promoting transparency, addressing concerns, and framing AI as an opportunity for growth, not replacement.

- **Align AI projects with business strategy** to ensure that AI initiatives support the organization's overall goals and drive long-term value.

Chapter 5: AI Leadership and Decision Making

Successful AI projects require **visionary leadership** that is aligned with the company's strategic goals. It's not enough for leaders to merely support AI initiatives from the top down. They need to be actively involved in driving the transformation, making informed decisions about AI, and leading their teams through the inevitable challenges that arise along the way.

AI is often perceived as a **technical endeavour**, driven by data scientists and machine learning engineers. But, as Sarah learned, AI is just as much about people as it is about algorithms. It requires leadership to ensure that AI projects are aligned with business objectives, that cross-functional teams collaborate effectively, and that there is a culture of continuous learning and adaptation. Leaders are not just decision-makers—they are the visionaries who shape how AI can transform the organization, ensuring that it delivers long-term value.

Let's dive into the role of leadership in driving AI transformation and how leaders can make **informed, data-driven decisions** that position their organizations for success.

Balancing Short-Term Goals with Long-Term AI Strategy

One of the most significant challenges Sarah faced was balancing her company's short-term goals with a long-term AI strategy. AI has the potential to revolutionize every aspect of business, from marketing and operations to customer service and product development. But AI is not a "quick fix." It requires time, resources, and a long-term commitment to build out the necessary infrastructure, talent, and tools to make it successful.

For Sarah, this meant that AI projects had to deliver value early on while also setting the foundation for long-term success. At first, the company used **predictive analytics** to personalize marketing campaigns, which resulted in quick wins—higher conversion rates and improved customer engagement. These initial successes were essential in building momentum for AI adoption, but Sarah knew that this was just the beginning.

While the short-term results were important, Sarah kept her eye on the bigger picture. She recognized that AI's true potential could only be realized if it was integrated into every aspect of the business, from supply chain optimization to automation of customer service processes. She worked with her leadership team to develop a **roadmap for scaling AI** that aligned with the company's long-term vision. This strategy would allow the company to start small, achieve quick wins, and then expand AI projects as they demonstrated success.

The key to this approach was **iterative progress**. AI adoption is a journey, not a destination. Leaders need to ensure that the company's AI strategy is flexible, adaptable, and can scale as the organization learns and grows.

Example: Consider **John**, the CFO of a manufacturing company, who was faced with a similar challenge. John knew that AI could streamline operations and reduce costs, but he also had to show immediate ROI to the company's investors. John began by implementing AI in predictive maintenance, which quickly saved the company money by preventing unplanned machine downtime. This was a short-term success that validated the AI approach. Over time, John expanded AI into other areas, like inventory management and supply chain optimization, which provided long-term value for the business.

Understanding the Ethical Implications of AI Decisions

AI's ability to make **autonomous decisions** can be both empowering and challenging for leaders. Unlike traditional systems, where humans have full control over decision-making, AI systems often make decisions based on **algorithms** that learn from data, sometimes making decisions that may be difficult for humans to explain. This is particularly important when AI is used in areas like **finance**, **healthcare**, or **human resources**, where decisions can directly impact people's lives.

For example, Sarah's company used AI to personalize marketing campaigns by predicting which products customers were likely to purchase next. While this was an incredibly effective tool, Sarah knew that she had to ensure the algorithm wasn't unintentionally creating biased or unfair recommendations. She needed to make sure that her AI system was **transparent** and **ethical**, ensuring that it was fair, unbiased, and aligned with the company's values.

To do this, Sarah worked with her AI team to implement **ethical guidelines** for AI development. They used tools for **explainable AI (XAI)**, which allowed them to understand and explain how decisions were made by the algorithm. They also set up processes to **regularly audit the AI models** for any signs of bias, ensuring that the models were continuously optimized and aligned with ethical standards.

Leaders need to consider the **broader implications of AI** on society, employees, and customers. As AI systems are integrated into business processes, it's crucial to **establish strong governance** around the use of AI and ensure that all AI models comply with **ethical principles** and **regulatory guidelines**.

Case Study: A **financial services company** used AI to determine credit scores for loan applicants. However, they soon realized that the AI models were unintentionally discriminating against certain groups of applicants due to biased data. The company implemented a rigorous auditing process and leveraged explainable AI techniques to identify the bias in the system. By doing so, they were able to adjust the algorithm and restore fairness in their decision-making process, ultimately improving both customer satisfaction and regulatory compliance.

Leading with Empathy: Building Trust Around AI

As AI becomes more embedded in business operations, employees and customers alike may feel uncertain about how these systems work and whether they can trust the decisions they make. This is why leadership in AI adoption is not only about strategic vision and technical expertise but also about building **trust** and fostering **transparency** within the organization.

Sarah understood that her employees needed to feel confident in the AI systems they were using and, most importantly, that they were part of the **AI transformation** process. To build this trust, Sarah engaged her teams early on. She made sure that they understood the potential benefits of AI—not just in terms of productivity, but also in how AI could improve their day-to-day work. For example, Sarah's customer service team was initially sceptical about AI-driven chatbots, fearing they would be replaced. But Sarah explained that the chatbots would only handle simple inquiries, allowing her team to focus on more complex customer interactions.

Empathy was key to building trust. Sarah listened to concerns, addressed fears, and provided clear, transparent communication throughout the AI adoption process. She emphasized that AI was there to **enhance human capabilities**, not replace them. This open dialogue helped to shift the company's mindset about AI from fear to opportunity.

Leaders must also focus on **building relationships** with customers and clients, ensuring they understand how AI is being used and how their data is protected. AI transparency builds customer trust, particularly in industries like finance, healthcare, and retail, where customers expect ethical use of their data.

Example: In the healthcare industry, AI is being used to help doctors diagnose diseases, but there is often scepticism about the accuracy of AI-powered diagnoses. **Dr. Susan**, a hospital administrator, made sure that her team of doctors and nurses was involved in the decision-making process. She hosted workshops where AI experts explained how the AI models worked and how their diagnoses were validated by medical professionals. This transparent communication helped the medical staff trust the AI system, resulting in more efficient diagnoses and better patient outcomes.

Empowering Data-Driven Decision Making

One of the key benefits of AI is that it enables **data-driven decision-making**. By leveraging AI models, businesses can base their decisions on hard data, rather than intuition or guesswork. AI can analyse massive datasets in real-time and offer insights that would be impossible for a human to uncover on their own.

Sarah's leadership team embraced this aspect of AI as they moved forward with their initiatives. By using predictive analytics, they were able to forecast trends in customer demand and optimize inventory levels, making data-backed decisions that improved efficiency and customer satisfaction. Sarah empowered her team to use AI to drive decisions, ensuring that all decisions were supported by data, not assumptions.

Example:
In the retail industry, AI-driven analytics are being used to predict demand, optimize pricing, and personalize shopping experiences. For instance, **Wendy**, the chief marketing officer of a global retail brand, used AI to analyse customer purchasing data and predict when shoppers would make their next purchase. With this data, Wendy's team could offer personalized promotions at just the right time, significantly increasing conversion rates.

Strategic Decision Making: Aligning AI with Business Goals

As AI becomes an integral part of business strategy, it's essential for leaders to ensure that AI initiatives are aligned with the company's long-term goals. AI shouldn't be seen as a separate project, but as a **core component of the business strategy**. Whether the goal is to increase revenue, improve operational efficiency, or enhance customer experience, AI should serve as a tool to help achieve those objectives.

Sarah regularly revisited her **AI roadmap** with her leadership team to ensure that each AI initiative supported the company's overall strategy. She made sure that all AI projects were focused on **solving real business problems** and delivering measurable outcomes.

Key Takeaways:

- **Leadership** is crucial in driving AI transformation. Leaders must guide their organizations through AI adoption with clear vision, alignment, and engagement.

- **Balance short-term wins** with long-term AI strategies. AI is an ongoing journey that requires iterative progress and flexibility.

- **Ethical considerations** are critical in AI. Leaders must ensure that AI systems are fair, transparent, and aligned with the company's values.

- **Empathy and transparency** are key to building trust in AI. Leaders should engage employees and customers in the AI adoption process, addressing their concerns and emphasizing AI's role in enhancing human capabilities.

- **Data-driven decision-making** empowers leaders to make smarter, more informed choices. AI should be used to align business strategies and deliver tangible outcomes.

Chapter 6: Navigating AI Implementation Challenges

While AI holds immense potential, **implementation is rarely smooth sailing**. AI adoption is not just about deploying new technology; it requires careful planning, adaptation, and the ability to solve real-world problems as they arise. Sarah, the CEO of the e-commerce company, found this out firsthand. Even after her company had done the hard work of building an AI-ready organization—aligning leadership, creating the right data infrastructure, and fostering a culture of innovation—she faced a new set of challenges when it came time to implement AI.

Like many business leaders, Sarah realized that implementing AI is rarely straightforward. From data quality issues to the complexities of integrating AI with existing systems, there are a multitude of **hurdles** that can slow down AI adoption and prevent it from delivering the expected outcomes. However, what sets successful companies apart is their ability to anticipate these challenges, **address them head-on**, and adjust their strategies as needed.

This chapter will explore the most common challenges in AI implementation and provide **practical strategies** for overcoming them.

Challenge 1: Data Quality and Availability

One of the first obstacles Sarah encountered was the issue of **data quality**. While her company had accumulated a wealth of data, it was fragmented, inconsistent, and often incomplete. AI models depend on large volumes of high-quality data, and any gaps or inaccuracies can lead to poor model performance. Sarah's team faced the daunting task of cleaning and organizing this data to ensure it was ready for AI use.

Data quality is a persistent challenge in AI adoption. Without clean, structured data, AI models cannot make accurate predictions or generate actionable insights. This is why building a solid **data foundation** is crucial for any AI project.

Solution: Sarah invested heavily in **data governance** practices. She set up a team to audit the data, identify gaps, and clean the data to ensure consistency and accuracy. This process involved:

- **Data standardization**: Converting data into a uniform format across departments.

- **Data cleansing**: Identifying and removing errors or inconsistencies in the data.

- **Data validation**: Ensuring that the data is complete and accurate before feeding it into AI models.

By addressing these issues early on, Sarah was able to provide her AI models with the high-quality data they needed to succeed. In addition, she set up **data pipelines** that allowed her company to automate the process of gathering, cleaning, and storing data in real-time, making it easier to scale AI projects across the organization.

Example:
A **retail company** faced similar challenges when trying to deploy AI for personalized marketing. Their customer data was spread across multiple systems, with incomplete records and inconsistent formatting. The company brought in **data engineers** to create a centralized data repository and implemented a robust data governance framework. With clean, validated data, their AI model for personalized recommendations significantly improved customer engagement and sales.

Challenge 2: Overcoming Technical Debt and Integration Issues

Another significant challenge Sarah faced was the **integration of AI** into existing business systems and processes. Her company had several legacy systems in place, each operating in silos. The AI models her team developed required integration with these systems to make real-time decisions, update inventory levels, and deliver personalized customer recommendations.

But **legacy systems** were not designed with AI in mind and connecting them to newer technologies posed several hurdles. Sarah's team had to re-engineer parts of their infrastructure to make the AI integration seamless. The process was complex, time-consuming, and required careful coordination between the technical and business teams.

Solution: The key to overcoming integration challenges is taking a **modular approach** to AI implementation. Rather than trying to overhaul the entire IT infrastructure at once, Sarah's team chose to focus on specific use cases where AI could deliver immediate value. They worked with the IT department to ensure that the AI models could be integrated with existing systems without causing significant disruptions. By focusing on **pilot projects**, Sarah's team was able to test AI in a controlled environment and identify potential integration issues before scaling them across the business.

Example:

A **healthcare provider** faced a similar issue when trying to implement AI-driven diagnostics tools alongside their existing electronic health record (EHR) systems. The EHR systems were outdated and not compatible with AI tools. The organization chose to integrate AI in phases, starting with a **cloud-based solution** that could communicate with the EHR system via APIs. This allowed the AI to run diagnostics and provide recommendations without needing a complete overhaul of their infrastructure.

Challenge 3: Ethical Concerns, Privacy Issues, and Regulatory Compliance

As AI becomes more embedded in business processes, **ethical concerns**—particularly around **data privacy**—become increasingly important. Sarah's company collected vast amounts of customer data, and with that came the responsibility to protect it. Customers are more aware than ever of how their data is being used, and businesses must comply with **data privacy regulations** such as the **General Data Protection Regulation (GDPR)** in Europe and the **California Consumer Privacy Act (CCPA)** in the United States.

In addition to privacy concerns, AI can sometimes produce biased or discriminatory outcomes if not carefully managed. This is especially true in **decision-making systems** like credit scoring, hiring algorithms, and predictive analytics. AI models are only as good as the data they are trained on, and if the data is biased, the AI system will be as well.

Solution: To address these ethical challenges, Sarah set up an **AI ethics committee** that included legal, compliance, and data science experts. The committee's role was to ensure that AI projects complied with data privacy regulations and ethical standards. Sarah also implemented tools for **explainable AI (XAI)**, which allowed her team to better understand how the AI models made decisions and ensure they were free from bias.

Example:

A **financial institution** used AI for loan approval decisions. However, after deploying the model, the institution found that it was inadvertently discriminating against certain demographic groups. The company hired an external **audit team** to evaluate the model's fairness and ensure that it complied with **fair lending laws**. After identifying the biases, they adjusted the model and incorporated fairness constraints into its design to ensure equitable outcomes.

Challenge 4: Managing Stakeholder Expectations

AI projects can take time to deliver results, and stakeholders often expect immediate returns on their investments. Sarah's leadership team was eager to see quick improvements in customer retention and sales, but the reality of AI adoption was that it required time to build, train, and test models before they could deliver measurable outcomes.

This led to **misaligned expectations** at times, especially when the initial results weren't as strong as anticipated. For instance, the marketing team expected AI-driven recommendations to immediately drive a large increase in conversion rates, but it took several months of refinement to get the model to the point where it was consistently generating high-quality predictions.

Solution: Sarah understood the importance of **managing expectations** and communicating openly with stakeholders. She worked with her leadership team to set realistic timelines and demonstrate that AI projects are often iterative. Rather than focusing on short-term success, she encouraged her team to celebrate the incremental improvements along the way.

To further align expectations, Sarah made sure that stakeholders were involved throughout the project's lifecycle. Regular **check-ins** with the leadership team helped keep everyone informed about the progress of AI initiatives, the challenges faced, and the roadmap for future improvements.

Example:

A **logistics company** was implementing AI to optimize delivery routes. While the AI model showed initial promise, it took time for it to be fine-tuned and to adapt to the real-world complexities of the delivery network. The company's leadership communicated openly with stakeholders, emphasizing that AI was an ongoing process of learning and improvement. As the model was optimized over time, it led to significant reductions in fuel costs and delivery times.

Challenge 5: Overcoming Resistance to AI Adoption

Change is difficult, and **resistance to AI adoption** is common, especially when employees feel their jobs may be threatened by automation. Sarah faced this resistance head-on by emphasizing the benefits of AI for both the company and its employees.

One of the major concerns her team had was the fear that AI would replace jobs. Sarah knew that AI wasn't meant to replace people, but to enhance their work by automating repetitive tasks and enabling them to focus on higher-value, strategic tasks. For example, AI-powered chatbots could handle routine customer inquiries, freeing up customer service agents to focus on complex issues that required human empathy and problem-solving skills.

Solution: Sarah took a **collaborative approach** to overcoming resistance. She involved employees in the AI adoption process, explaining how AI would complement their work rather than replace it. Sarah also **upskilled her employees**, providing training programs that helped them learn how to work with AI tools. This not only empowered employees but also made them feel like active participants in the AI transformation.

Example:
At a **manufacturing plant**, workers were concerned that AI-driven robots would replace their jobs. However, the company's leadership worked closely with the workforce to explain that the

robots would handle repetitive tasks, allowing workers to focus on quality control and problem-solving. The company also provided training to help workers operate and maintain the robots, empowering them to embrace AI as a tool that enhanced their roles.

Key Takeaways:

- **Data quality** is foundational for successful AI adoption. Invest in data governance and ensure your data is clean, structured, and accessible.

- Overcome **integration challenges** by taking a modular approach and addressing legacy system incompatibilities in manageable stages.

- Address **ethical concerns and privacy issues** by implementing AI governance, ensuring compliance with data regulations, and monitoring for bias in AI models.

- **Manage stakeholder expectations** by setting realistic timelines, celebrating small wins, and keeping stakeholders informed throughout the process.

- Overcome **resistance to AI** by emphasizing AI's role in enhancing, not replacing, human jobs and by providing opportunities for upskilling.

Chapter 7: The Future of AI in Business and Leadership

As Sarah continued to witness the ongoing transformation within her company, she began to recognize that AI adoption was not a one-time event—it was a dynamic, **evolving journey**. AI was changing the way her company operated, but it was also changing the broader landscape of business. The applications of AI were growing beyond traditional uses in predictive analytics, customer service, and process automation. New AI innovations were emerging at a rapid pace, opening new possibilities that Sarah hadn't anticipated when she first embarked on her AI journey.

The technology landscape is evolving in real-time. While AI technologies like machine learning and natural language processing (NLP) are now widely used, we are on the cusp of even greater changes. Innovations like **Generative AI**, **autonomous systems**, and **edge computing** are poised to redefine what AI can do for businesses. Sarah knew that to stay ahead of the curve, she needed to not only be aware of these emerging technologies but also actively prepare her organization to leverage them for long-term competitive advantage.

For leaders, the question isn't just how to implement AI today—it's how to position their organizations to thrive in an AI-driven future. This means anticipating future trends, embracing continuous innovation, and fostering a **growth mindset** within their teams.

AI and the Next Frontier: Emerging Technologies

AI is evolving rapidly, and the technologies that are on the horizon promise to revolutionize industries and business operations in profound ways. Some of the most exciting developments include:

Generative AI (GenAI)

Generative AI is a game-changer. Unlike traditional AI models that analyse existing data to make predictions or automate tasks, **Generative AI** creates entirely new content. This can include **text**, **images**, **videos**, and even **music** or **software code**.

One of the most well-known examples of GenAI is **GPT-4** (the model behind this very conversation), which generates highly coherent and contextually accurate text based on a given prompt. But the implications of generative AI go far beyond content creation. Businesses are increasingly using GenAI to assist in product design, **creative writing**, **video generation**, and **automated coding**.

Sarah's Insight: Sarah saw the potential of **Generative AI** for content marketing. Rather than relying solely on a team of writers, her marketing department could use AI to generate **product descriptions**, **social media posts**, and even **video scripts**. This not only saved time but allowed her team to focus on strategy, creativity, and customer engagement. Sarah also realized that GenAI could be a valuable tool in **product development**, where AI could propose design concepts or generate innovative solutions based on customer data.

As businesses like Sarah's begun to adopt GenAI, we will see a surge in content automation, personalized communications, and even the creation of new digital products. **Creative industries** will be among the first to benefit, but **GenAI** will soon permeate many sectors, offering efficiency, personalization, and innovation.

Autonomous Systems

Autonomous AI systems are machines that can perform complex tasks independently, often with little to no human intervention. These systems include **self-driving vehicles**, **drones**, and **robots** that navigate dynamic environments, make decisions, and perform tasks in real-time.

In industries like **logistics**, AI-driven autonomous vehicles and drones are already changing the way products are transported and delivered. Autonomous vehicles can reduce costs, improve delivery speeds, and reduce human error. In **manufacturing**, autonomous robots can improve production efficiency, perform hazardous tasks, and even collaborate with human workers.

Sarah began to consider how **autonomous systems** could play a role in her own business. Could her company use AI-powered delivery drones to speed up the last-mile delivery of customer orders? Could robots in warehouses help automate packaging and reduce the need for manual labour?

The future of autonomous systems is **multidimensional**—they have applications across **transportation**, **manufacturing**, **healthcare**, and even **agriculture**. For leaders, this presents new opportunities to automate tasks that were once thought of as manual or human-driven, significantly enhancing productivity and reducing operational costs.

Edge Computing and Real-Time AI

One of the challenges with traditional cloud-based AI solutions is **latency**—the delay between data collection and decision-making. In today's fast-paced world, many AI applications require **real-time data processing** to make timely decisions. This is where **edge computing** comes into play. Edge computing involves processing data **locally**, on devices or sensors, instead of sending it to a centralized server for analysis.

Edge AI allows businesses to process data closer to the source, whether that's a **smart factory**, **autonomous vehicle**, or **retail store**. This reduces latency, increases operational speed, and enhances decision-making in **real-time**.

Example: A **smart factory** could use edge AI to monitor production lines, detect defects in real-time, and immediately adjust machinery settings to maintain quality. This reduces downtime and improves overall efficiency.

For leaders, this means preparing their organizations to leverage **edge computing** for applications that require immediate, data-driven decision-making. Whether it's in **supply chain optimization**, **predictive maintenance**, or **customer interactions**, edge AI will enable faster and more agile responses to dynamic conditions.

AI-Driven Predictive Analytics

Predictive analytics has become a core application of AI. However, the next generation of AI-driven predictive models will be **far more accurate**, **granular**, and **context-aware**. By leveraging vast amounts of data and advanced algorithms, AI will predict not just general trends but also highly specific, real-time behaviours and needs.

In retail, for example, AI will predict not only which products customers are likely to purchase but also **when** they will need them, **how much** they will buy, and **how** they want the product delivered. This **hyper-personalization** will make marketing, inventory management, and customer service much more targeted and efficient.

For Sarah's business, predictive analytics could help forecast customer demand more accurately, optimize inventory levels, and even anticipate trends before they hit the market. This proactive, **data-driven decision-making** will be a key differentiator for businesses looking to stay ahead of the competition.

Preparing for AI in the Long-Term: Building a Sustainable AI Strategy

As AI continues to evolve, business leaders must shift their focus from short-term implementation to long-term sustainability. To build a **future-proof AI strategy**, leaders must take a holistic approach that considers not only the **technology** but also the **people**, **processes**, and **governance** needed to support AI adoption in the long run.

Upskilling and Reskilling the Workforce

The **future of work** will be shaped by AI, but **humans will still play a crucial role**. As AI automates repetitive tasks, employees will be freed up to focus on higher-value work. However, to truly leverage AI, organizations will need to invest in **upskilling and reskilling** their workforce.

Sarah's Commitment to Upskilling: Sarah was proactive in providing training for her employees, ensuring that they not only understood how to work with AI but were also equipped to adapt to new roles and responsibilities. Her AI academy helped employees learn everything from the basics of machine learning to advanced topics like neural networks and deep learning.

Example:
A **global technology company** invested in upskilling programs

that taught employees how to develop, manage, and operate AI systems. This helped bridge the talent gap and ensured that employees could continue to innovate and collaborate with AI-driven systems.

AI Governance and Ethical Standards

As AI becomes more embedded in business operations, the need for strong **governance** becomes more pressing. Organizations must implement clear **AI governance frameworks** that ensure ethical AI usage, **data privacy**, and **accountability**.

AI Ethics and Responsibility: Leaders must set the tone by ensuring AI systems are **transparent**, **fair**, and **aligned** with the company's values. They must also ensure that the **data used in AI models** is unbiased, representative, and compliant with privacy laws like **GDPR** or **CCPA**.

Sarah set up an **AI ethics committee** within her organization to ensure that her AI initiatives adhered to the highest ethical standards. This committee was responsible for auditing models for bias, ensuring transparency in decision-making, and upholding the company's commitment to responsible AI.

Building a Long-Term AI Roadmap

Developing an AI strategy is not a one-time task—it's a journey. Sarah worked with her leadership team to create a **long-term roadmap** for AI adoption. This roadmap included:

1. Identifying **key AI use cases** aligned with the company's long-term goals.

2. Setting **milestones** to measure progress and adjust the AI strategy as needed.

3. Ensuring **scalability** by gradually expanding AI initiatives across departments.

4. Continuously monitoring **performance metrics** to ensure AI projects deliver measurable business value.

The roadmap was designed to be **flexible**, allowing Sarah's company to adapt to new AI developments, customer demands, and market shifts.

Preparing for an AI-Driven Future: Building Adaptability

In an era of **rapid technological change**, **adaptability** is the key to survival. The business landscape will continue to evolve, and companies that succeed will be those that can quickly **pivot**, **experiment**, and **embrace change**. AI will continue to transform industries, and leaders must foster an environment where experimentation is encouraged, risks are managed, and innovation thrives.

Sarah recognized that **building an adaptable organization** meant creating a culture of **continuous learning**, where employees were not only encouraged to embrace new technologies but were also equipped to **drive innovation** within the company. This agility would allow her organization to remain competitive in the fast-changing world of AI.

Example:
A **leading logistics company** created a culture of **innovation** by implementing an AI "innovation lab," where employees could experiment with

new AI-driven technologies, pilot new solutions, and collaborate across departments. This initiative allowed the company to stay ahead of the competition and drive continuous improvements in their AI strategy.

Key Takeaways:

- **Emerging AI technologies**, such as Generative AI, autonomous systems, and edge computing, will shape the future of business, offering new opportunities for innovation and growth.

- Leaders must develop a **long-term AI strategy** that includes **continuous upskilling**, **strong governance**, and the ability to **adapt to new technologies**.

- **AI governance** and ethical frameworks are essential for ensuring that AI is used responsibly, transparently, and in line with company values.

- **Building an adaptable culture** is critical for long-term AI success, enabling organizations to quickly pivot and experiment as AI technologies evolve.

Chapter 8: Conclusion – Leading AI-Driven Change

As you read through the chapters of this book, we've explored how AI can **revolutionize operations**, enhance **customer experiences**, and drive **measurable value**. We've examined the challenges and opportunities of AI adoption, the importance of leadership alignment, and the ways in which AI is reshaping industries.

But as you close this chapter, there is one fundamental truth that stands out: **the future of AI is not defined by technology alone—it is defined by leadership**. To truly harness AI's transformative potential, leaders must step up, guide their teams, and **take responsibility for driving AI-driven change**.

The Roadmap for AI Adoption: From Strategy to Execution

The journey of AI adoption is a dynamic and ongoing process. As we've seen through Sarah's story, the key to successful AI adoption lies in **visionary leadership**, **clear goals**, and a willingness to embrace change. AI will continue to evolve, and business leaders need to stay ahead of the curve by **adapting** and **innovating** at every stage.

Here is a **roadmap** for leaders as they move forward with their AI initiatives:

1. **Start with a Clear Vision**:

    o **Understand the role of AI** in your industry and how it can benefit your business.

    o Define your **AI goals** based on your long-term business strategy. Are you looking to improve efficiency, enhance customer experiences, or drive innovation?

    o Establish **success metrics** early on so that you can measure the tangible impact of AI initiatives.

2. **Create an AI-Ready Organization**:

    o Assess your organization's **readiness for AI** in terms of data infrastructure, culture, and talent.

    o Ensure that your team is **aligned** and that the right leaders are in place to champion AI projects.

    o Build a culture that encourages **innovation**, **collaboration**, and **continuous learning**. AI is an ongoing journey, and your team should feel empowered to experiment and adapt.

3. **Focus on People, Process, and Technology**:

    o **Upskill your workforce** to ensure that employees have the AI skills they need to collaborate with technology effectively.

    o Invest in **the right technology**, ensuring that your data infrastructure supports AI initiatives.

    o Focus on **change management**, addressing concerns and **building trust** with employees and customers. People need to understand how AI will enhance their work, not replace it.

4. **Scale AI Gradually**:

    o Start with **small pilot projects** that can generate quick wins and demonstrate the value of AI.

    o Use these early projects to build momentum and **validate the technology** before expanding to larger initiatives.

- Continuously **optimize and iterate** on AI models based on feedback and performance metrics.

5. **Lead with Empathy and Ethical Standards**:

    - Address the **ethical implications** of AI in decision-making and ensure that AI models are fair, transparent, and accountable.

    - Lead with **empathy**, engaging your employees and stakeholders in open discussions about the opportunities and challenges AI brings.

    - Establish clear **governance frameworks** to ensure that AI is being used responsibly and aligns with your company's values.

6. **Monitor Progress and Adapt**:

    - AI is not a "set-and-forget" solution—it requires ongoing **monitoring and optimization**.

    - Regularly review AI performance and assess whether the technology is meeting the defined **KPIs** and **business goals**.

- Be prepared to pivot and adapt based on **new developments** in AI technology and evolving market conditions.

The Role of AI Leadership in the Future

Leaders must be visionaries who not only understand the potential of AI but are also prepared to guide their organizations through the complexities of implementation. They must be **strategic, empowering their teams,** and **fostering a culture of continuous learning**. AI is not just for technical teams; it's a business strategy that requires a collective effort across the entire organization.

Sarah, like many other leaders, has learned that **leading AI-driven change is about empowering others**—giving teams the tools, resources, and autonomy to drive innovation and create value with AI. Leaders must **build trust** by being transparent, addressing concerns, and ensuring that AI is used ethically. At the same time, they must **champion AI adoption** and align it with broader business goals to ensure long-term success.

As AI continues to evolve, **leaders will need to adapt their strategies** to leverage new AI innovations and integrate them into their business models. The AI-driven future will be shaped by leaders who are agile, open to experimentation, and focused on delivering value for customers, employees, and shareholders alike.

Taking Charge of AI-Driven Change

Now that you've learned about the key components of AI adoption—from setting a clear vision to scaling AI projects and overcoming challenges—it's time to act. The future of AI is filled with immense opportunities, but only those who are prepared to lead, innovate, and drive change will succeed. As you move forward, consider the following:

- **Embrace AI as a strategic priority**: Don't treat AI as a one-off project, but as an ongoing, evolving journey that is central to your organization's growth and success.

- **Lead by example**: As a leader, your actions set the tone for the rest of the organization. Embrace AI, invest in it, and champion its potential.

- **Encourage innovation at all levels**: AI is not just for the IT department; it's for everyone. Encourage your teams to experiment, collaborate, and use AI to solve real business challenges.

- **Commit to continuous learning**: AI is a rapidly evolving field. Keep learning, stay informed, and ensure that your team is constantly improving and adapting.

- **Be transparent and ethical**: AI is a powerful tool, but it comes with great responsibility. Ensure that your AI systems are fair, transparent, and aligned with your company's ethical standards.

AI is already reshaping the way businesses operate, but the journey has only just begun. The leaders who will succeed are those who **embrace AI's potential**, take bold action, and lead their teams through this transformative change.

The journey of AI adoption is one of continuous learning, experimentation, and transformation. But it is also a journey that can lead to tremendous rewards. By embracing AI, you're not only positioning your company to succeed in the future—you're also fostering an environment of **innovation**, **growth**, and **ethical leadership** that will sustain your organization for years to come.

As a leader, you have the power to shape the future of AI in your organization. **Take charge, lead with vision**, and set your company on a path toward a brighter, more AI-driven future.

The future of AI is now—and it's yours to shape.

Key Takeaways:

- **Lead AI adoption as a strategic priority**—AI is not just a technology, but a transformative business tool.

- **Champion AI adoption** by aligning teams, setting clear goals, and continuously adapting your strategy to new developments.

- **Foster a culture of innovation** and empower employees at all levels to engage with AI.

- **Commit to ethical AI** by ensuring transparency, fairness, and accountability in AI systems.

- **Embrace continuous learning**—AI is evolving, and so must your leadership approach.

Acknowledgement

I would like to take a moment to express my heartfelt gratitude to those who have supported me throughout this journey. A special thank you goes to my beloved wife, Maryam. Your unconditional support and love have been my guiding light through every difficulty and challenge. You have stood by me with unwavering strength and encouragement, believing in me even when I struggled to believe in myself. Your patience and understanding have made this journey possible, and I am endlessly grateful to have you by my side. Thank you for inspiring me every day and for being my partner in life and in dreams.

With all my love, Hamid

About The Author

My name is Hamid Oudi, and my life has been shaped by experiences of change, growth, and a desire to make meaningful contributions. I was born in Iran and moved to the United Kingdom in 2006 as a child. Adjusting to a new country with a different language and culture was a significant challenge, but it also taught me resilience, adaptability, and the value of curiosity.

These experiences inspired me to write *The Curious Journey of Biscuit Boy*. It's a simple, heartfelt story about transformation and finding one's place in the world—something I've experienced in my own journey. The story follows Biscuit Boy, a chocolate treat that comes to life, as he learns to navigate the world and discover his purpose. Writing this book allowed me to reflect on the lessons I've learned and share them in a way that's relatable and meaningful.

Professionally, I've always been drawn to technology and problem-solving. With a background in engineering and data science, I've spent my career exploring ways to use technology to make life easier and more efficient. As the director of MyFalcon Limited, I focus on designing systems that help businesses make better decisions using data and AI. My work has always been about finding practical solutions to real-world problems, and I'm grateful for the opportunities I've had to contribute to this field.

Sharing knowledge has also been an important part of my journey. I enjoy breaking down complex ideas and making them accessible, whether through my YouTube channel or conversations with others. Technology, to me, is a tool for empowerment, and I'm passionate about helping people and organizations use it to create positive change.

Looking back, I see my journey as one of gradual growth and learning. Moving to a new country taught me resilience and adaptability, while my work and writing have allowed me to contribute in small but meaningful ways. I still have much to learn and do, but I'm grateful for the path I've taken and excited for what lies ahead.

YouTube Channel at:

@myfalconuk

Printed in Great Britain
by Amazon